FEMALE SPORTS STARS

Michelle Kwan

Tara Lipinski

Superstars of Women's Basketball

Superstars of Women's Figure Skating

Superstars of Women's Golf

Superstars of Women's Gymnastics

Superstars of Women's Tennis

Superstars of Women's Track and Field

CHELSEA HOUSE PUBLISHERS

TARA LIPINSKI

Veda Boyd Jones

CHELSEA HOUSE PUBLISHERS
Philadelphia

CHELSEA HOUSE PUBLISHERS

Designed by Combined Books, Inc.
Conshohocken, Pennsylvania

Cover Illustration by Bonnie Gardner

1 3 5 7 9 8 6 4 2

Library of Congress Cataloguing-in-Publication Data

Jones, Veda Boyd.

      Tara Lipinski / Veda Boyd Jones.
         p.   cm.—(Female sports stars)
        Summary: Presents the success story of figure skater Tara
Lipinski, who at fourteen-years-old became the youngest
National Champion and World Champion in the history of
women's figure skating.
    ISBN 0-7910-4876-4 (hc)
     1. Lipinski, Tara, 1982- —Juvenile literature. 2. Skaters—
United States—Biography—Juvenile literature. 3. Women
skaters—United States—Biography—Juvenile literature.
[1. Lipinski, Tara, 1982- . 2. Ice skaters. 3. Women—
Biography.] I. Title. II. Series.
GV850.L56J65 1997
796.91'2'092—dc21
[B]   97-27734
                                           CIP
                                         AC

CONTENTS

At the Top

Fourteen-year-old Tara Lipinski, the youngest-ever U.S. National Figure Skating Champion, took a deep breath and stepped onto the ice when the announcer called her name.

She was in Lausanne, Switzerland, to compete in ladies' singles for the 1997 World Figure Skating Championship. Not only was she facing the best skaters from other countries, but she was the youngest in the competition.

A new rule by the International Skating Union (ISU) required competitors be at least 15 to compete at the world championships. Because Tara had competed in the Worlds in 1996, she was allowed to compete in 1997.

Music from the movie *Little Women* filled the rink. Tiny Tara, 4 feet 8 inches tall and 75

An exuberant Tara Lipinski skates during the Parade of Champions at the conclusion of the 1997 World Figure Skating Championships.

Skating with elegant spins and spirals, Tara would break the record set in 1927 by Sonja Henie by becoming the youngest World Figure Skating Champion ever.

pounds, with her light-brown hair pulled back in a bun to give her a more mature look, soared across the ice. She performed a perfect short program, which included six triple jumps that wowed the audience. Her graceful spins and fluid spirals combined with the triple jumps to bring the crowd to its feet.

By the end of the short program competition, which counted as one-third of the final score, Tara ranked first. Behind her, in second place, was Vanessa Gusmeroli, an 18-year-old from France. Maria Butyrskaya, 24, of Russia was third.

The defending world champion, 16-year-old Michelle Kwan, also from the United States, was in fourth place. Michelle had stumbled during the triple Lutz jump, the only mistake in her program, but it proved costly.

The other member of the United States delegation to the Worlds, 19-year-old Nicole Bobek, fell apart on the ice. Her skating coach, Carlo Fassi, had died of a heart attack at a local hospital the day before. Understandably, Nicole's concentration was dulled. She had only three hours of sleep before her short program. She placed eighth after stumbling during one jump and falling on another.

At the end of the short programs, Tara Lipinski was on top. What if she won on Saturday night?

In the past five years, there had been five different world champions. If Tara won, there would be six in six years. The youngest world champion had been Sonja Henie of Norway, and Tara was a month younger than Sonja was when she won in 1927.

A record was at stake. More importantly, her chance at the Olympics was at stake. Fifteen of the last 18 women who had been world champions the year before the Winter Olympics had gone on to win the gold.

That was Tara's dream. But the long program represented two-thirds of the score. If any of the other three finalists placed first in this part of the competition, Tara would sink to third place. She wouldn't become the world champion.

During the long program, Vanessa Gusmeroli touched the ice to prevent herself from falling on her first jump, and none of her four triple jumps were in difficult combinations.

Before her four-minute program, Tara paced nervously outside the rink. Dressed in white lace, her hair again in a bun, she wore a favorite necklace with a charm that said "Short but Good." When her name was called, she smiled and determinedly skated onto the ice.

She jumped, she twirled, she spun to music from the soundtracks of the movies *Sense and Sensibility* and *Much Ado About Nothing.* She landed her difficult triple loop–triple loop jump combination. She made no mistakes. At the end of her program, she again earned a standing ovation. Her marks from the nine judges were 5.8s and 5.9s out of possible 6.0s for technical merit. She was judged slightly lower on artistic

Having gone into the free program in first place, Tara reacts with relief at the end of her near perfect performance at the 1997 World Figure Skating Championship.

presentation and received one 5.7 and one 5.6.

The judges had left room for the others to win.

Russian Maria Butyrskaya ran out of energy before her long program ended and didn't attempt many difficult jumps.

But Michelle Kwan easily landed the combination jump that had given her trouble in the short program. She displayed elegance and poise in her performance as an Indian princess at the Taj Mahal. Her beautiful spins and spirals and graceful movements earned her 5.9s for artistic presentation.

The last skater, Irina Slutskaya, the 18-year-old from Russia who had finished sixth in the short program, could figure significantly in the rankings. If she finished second in the long program, it would knock Tara down to third. Michelle Kwan would retain her title. Irina hit her six triple jumps, but she left out a planned jump at the end of her program. Although she scored high, it wasn't high enough.

Tara finished second in the long program behind Michelle Kwan, but the judges were split on the final tally. Three put Tara first, three voted for Michelle, and three gave Irina first place. It came down to those tenths of a point in the short and the long programs. When they were all added up, history was made.

On March 22, 1997, Tara Lipinski became

the youngest ladies' World Figure Skating Champion. She was 14 years, nine months, and 12 days old.

Michelle Kwan was awarded the silver medal. The United States had finished first and second. Vanessa Gusmeroli of France received the bronze medal.

"I never expected to win, not this year," Tara said to the press after she won the gold medal. "It was a big shock. But I love it."

TARA'S PASSION

Tara's skating career started on roller skates in Sewell, New Jersey. The small suburb is across the Delaware River from Philadelphia, Pennsylvania, where Tara was born at Methodist Hospital on June 10, 1982.

At three, she learned to balance on four wheels and scoot around a roller rink. Soon, she was taking lessons and learning to jump and spin. Two years later, she won a regional competition.

When she was six, in first grade, her parents took her ice skating. Jack and Patricia Lipinski went inside for hot chocolate and discussed how Tara was not a natural on ice. In the first few minutes, she had slipped and fallen before clinging tightly to the rail. When they returned, though, they found a different Tara.

Skating from the age of six, Tara put years of practice and sacrifice into perfecting her grace and skills on the ice. Ice skating became her life.

"She had transferred everything she knew from roller-skating," her mother said, "and was doing jumps and turns on the ice."

And Tara loved it.

Her parents bought her a horse to discourage her obsession for ice skating. It didn't work. What about piano? No, that wasn't as exciting as floating on air in a jump or speeding across the ice. What about the fun of being a model? No, nothing could match the exhilaration of ice skating.

Her parents remember that when Tara was six, she watched the 1988 Winter Olympics and was enthralled. She even stood on a box, pretending to be an Olympic medal winner. Now she had a goal and a way to succeed at that goal. Ice skating became her life.

When Tara began taking lessons at the University of Delaware in Newark, the United States Figure Skating Association, the governing body which sanctions Olympic-style skating, had different rules than it has today. Learning how to jump and twirl were fine, but there were levels of proficiency that had to be met. Tara had to pass tests before she could move through the ranks from juvenile to intermediate, novice, junior and, finally, to senior status.

The school figures, or compulsory figures, are a series of circles and complicated patterns on the ice. To learn those, Tara first had to know the basics of skating, and that included learning how to use the parts of skate blades.

There are several parts of a blade: an inside edge (the edge on the inside of the foot), an outside edge (the edge on the outside of the foot), and the middle (an eighth-of-an-inch thick area that is actually a groove between the two edges).

Both inside and outside edges have parts that enable the skater to skate forward or backward. At the front of the blade are teeth, called toe picks, that help a skater jump and spin.

Beginners skate flat or on the middle of the blade. Tara didn't stay a beginner long. She quickly learned to skate forward and backward on the edges of her skates. Next, she tried to hold an edge, or skate on one edge for a distance. If she held it long enough, she'd curve into a circle. The sharp edges of her skates cut into the ice, leaving a pattern.

The school figures that had to be learned to advance from one level of figure skating to the next were based on two or three linked circles. To begin, Tara skated on one foot, making a circle. This was the basic pattern.

Then she had to skate twice around the same circle, making patterns called tracings. A perfect figure was one in which the three lines are no more than a quarter of an inch apart. At test time, USFSA judges carried their clipboards and measuring tapes onto the ice to assess an ice skater's accuracy.

The intricate patterns were included in competitions. In the Olympic games, school figures accounted for 20 percent of the total score of a skater. The other 80 percent came from the short program, which required certain elements, and the longer freestyle skating program with the jumps and spins that Tara loved.

The school figures required good body control, concentration, strength, and patience. The figures were curves, and they demanded the control and accuracy necessary for the more advanced skating moves of jumps, spins, and complicated footwork.

In 1990, all that changed. The International

Skating Union, of which the USFSA was a national branch, voted to eliminate the school figures in competition because TV viewers were confused by the judging in Olympic figure skating events. They didn't like watching skaters slowly carve shapes into the ice. They wanted jumps, twirls, and graceful dancing. And they got it.

When the last skater at the 1990 World Figure Skating Championships completed her figures, judges examined etchings on ice for the last time. The school figures, from which figure skating got its name, were a thing of the past.

Tara delighted in the new rules for Olympic contenders. Her game was leaping, spiraling, and spinning. The challenge was to learn the compulsory moves that were required in the short program, which under the new rules now made up a third of a skater's total score.

Under the new Olympic regulations, eight technical elements were required in the two-minute and 40 second short program. They were: double Axel; double jump or triple jump; jump combination; flying spin; layback or sideways leaning spin; spin combination with only one change of foot and at least two changes of position; one spiral step sequence and another step sequence.

All of this could be performed in any order to music that Tara chose. Even though this was an event of required elements, it was scored on two levels: technical and artistic. The jumps and spins were important, but the skating also had to flow smoothly and gracefully and interpret the music.

Where to start? The double Axel was a complicated jump that Tara steered away from in the beginning. Other jumps, like the toe loop, were easier. The toe pick acted like a pole vault and helped with the takeoff.

This jump taught Tara the basic rotation position: legs crossed, arms retracted, and head over the left shoulder. For the toe loop, she took off from the right back outside edge of her skate, used her left toe pick to vault her into the air, made one revolution, and then landed on the right back outside edge.

It was a graceful jump when performed properly, and it made Tara look like she was floating on air. A double toe loop meant making two rotations in the air before landing. A triple meant making three turns. Of course, the more rotations, the more difficult the jump. But Tara rose to the challenge.

Learning to fall properly was as important as performing a successful jump. An injury could sideline Tara for months, and she wanted to skate, skate, skate. Whenever she fell to the side, she'd bend her knees and break the fall with her hands. She always got up quickly from a crawl position. No fall could keep Tara down for long.

Spins were always a crowd-pleaser, so Tara learned to spin like a whirling dervish. As she stepped into the camel spin, she leaned forward with an arched back and her chin raised. Her upper body was parallel to the ice with her arms held back and her free leg extended behind,

Learning the leaps, spirals, and spins of ice figure skating was very difficult work that took hours of practice every day. Tara thrived on the challenges.

Tara and her mother flew often between Delaware, where she trained, and Texas, where her father continued to live, working hard to support Tara's Olympic quest.

also parallel to the ice. This move, borrowed from ballet, showcased Tara's style.

A layback spin portrayed Tara's gracefulness. Here she leaned back with her free leg extended at a 45-degree angle. Correct positioning of her arms out to the side was important and again required the elegance of a ballerina.

The flying spins were not difficult for Tara because she had a solid spin technique and good jumping ability. For the flying sit spin, Tara combined a simple one rotation jump and came down in the sit position, with her skating leg fully bent and her free leg straight and turned out. Pointed toes were critical in earning good marks from judges, so Tara concentrated on those no matter what spin she worked on.

It was work. Practice, practice, practice. The more difficult a technical element, the more determined Tara became. If she couldn't master a movement, she concentrated harder. Her brown eyes would take on a steely look, and she'd repeat the movement again and again until she got it right. She thrived on repetition. The before-school and after-school sessions were the highlights of her day. She could skate for hours if allowed, but classwork and friends also made demands on her time.

Tara was coming along as a skater, showing great skills for a girl of nine, when her father was promoted to vice president and transferred to the Houston office of the Coastal Corporation, an energy company. In 1991, the family moved to Sugar Land, Texas.

Ice skating wasn't the big sport in Texas that it was in the Northeast, and the only place where Tara could continue to skate was the Ice Skating Center at the Galleria Mall. In December, Tara skated around a Christmas tree placed in the center of the ice as one of the mall's holiday decorations. She worked under coach Megan Faulkner in the skating school, but the center wasn't built as a training rink for future Olympic hopefuls. Tara would get up at 3:00 a.m. to rent the public rink so that she could train alone.

That type of devotion to the sport caused problems for her and her parents. A decision had to be made. Should Tara continue on her quest for Olympic gold? What was the best way to do that?

Tara's parents considered their options, then made a choice.

"What do you do when you have a kid who wants to do something so terribly badly?" her dad asked.

Her mother said, "She's happy, and when this is over, we can say we did what we thought was right. She can't imagine her life without skating."

Their family was already making a large financial investment in Tara's skating. Now they made a huge sacrifice. They refinanced the family home to support their decision, and Tara and her mother moved back East so Tara could train at the University of Delaware rink. Her father stayed in Texas, working hard to pay the bills.

PRACTICE, PRACTICE, PRACTICE

Life assumed a new kind of normal for Tara in 1993. She and her mother lived in a small apartment in Elkton, Maryland, just across the Delaware line and not far from the rink at the University of Delaware. She talked to her father on the phone, and he flew East to visit when he could. On holidays, she and her mother would fly to Texas.

After the fifth grade, she dropped out of school and continued her education with a tutor, Mrs. Keller, who came to the Lipinskis' apartment to teach her. Skating didn't leave a lot of time for the regulated hours of a normal school day. At home in the mornings, Tara studied science, math, reading, and English, her least favorite subject. Then, she'd change into her skating clothes.

Tara enthusiastically spent hours, days, weeks, years working toward her championship goals.

Because she needed freedom of movement, but protection from the cold of the rink, Tara wore tights and a practice dress with a turtle-neck sweater. She packed her skating bag with her skates, skate guards to put on her skates when she was off the ice, and skate covers, which she put on her skates after she'd taken them off for the day and dried the blades.

Tara didn't wear heavy socks with her skates. Although some skaters claimed they skated better with no socks at all, so they could feel the boot and feel the ice, Tara wore tights to keep her feet warm. She kept her well-fitted boots laced tightly.

On a typical day, her time at the ice rink in Newark, Delaware, was divided into sessions of around 40 or 45 minutes. First she'd take a lesson with her coach, Jeff DiGregorio. Mostly they would work on jumps.

For the Lutz jump, named after its inventor, Tara took off on her left back outside edge with a right toe-pick assist. She revolved counter-clockwise and landed on her right back outside edge.

After jumping over and over, Tara would take a rest break and talk with other skaters.

Her next session with Coach DiGregorio would focus on spins. These were among her favorites, and she prided herself on 20 to 25 rotations in one spin. After a brief rest period, she practiced on her own the jumps and spins that she'd learned in her lessons.

Lunch was normally mid-afternoon and eaten at the snack bar. A high-carbohydrate pasta was her usual choice.

Following lunch and after a warm-up period, she worked with her choreographer, Jill Cosgrove. The long program requires an artistic interpretation of music in addition to as many jumps and spins and spirals as a skater can physically handle.

The jumps were what impressed audiences, but the connecting footwork was also important. Tara worked on her arm and head movements and on memorizing her short and long programs. Her movements needed to correspond with the rhythm and tone and style of her background music. She also needed to use as much of the rink as possible, so her programs were a pattern of complex crisscrosses and large circles around the ice.

Next in her long day was another short break for a snack. Then she had a practice session on her long freestyle program with coach Ron Luddington.

The program had to be automatic for Tara so that she wouldn't forget any movement. If she fell, she got right up and continued the choreographed routine. It wouldn't do to stop the music and start over. In competition, the music went right on, and it was best for a skater to practice the program as if it were in front of judges. If Tara fell during the real thing, she'd have the confidence to continue the program as if nothing had gone wrong—showing poise under pressure.

In a typical day, Tara would spend around four hours on the ice. But her day wasn't over yet.

For the next hour, she'd take a ballet lesson with her coach Sergei. A figure skater must move with the grace of a ballerina, and Tara's ballet techniques made the physically difficult skating maneuvers look smooth and effortless. Judges would give her lower marks if her movements were abrupt and jerky.

And she always kept the judges in mind. After all, they would determine the path she took on her road to the Olympics. That was her goal, and she never lost sight of it.

Some days she lifted weights. Skating jumps required strong athletic ability, not only in her legs, but in her arms as well.

Back at home, after a hard day on the ice, Tara studied and did her homework just like a normal 11-year-old. But she would have rather been back on the ice. In her mind, she went over the jumps she was learning. Each one was different, and the liftoff techniques had to come automatically to her brain as well as to her body.

The loop jump was like the toe loop, except that she couldn't use the toe pick. Tara started the jump from the right back outside edge of her skate, made one revolution, and then landed on the right back outside edge. It wasn't the jump that was so difficult; it was getting three revolutions. To compete on the juniors' level, she needed at least three triple jumps.

The Salchow was also an edge jump; no help from the toe pick on this one either. Ulrich Salchow of Sweden invented this jump, and he was a world champion 10 times in the early 1900s.

For the Salchow, Tara took off from the left back inside edge of her skate, made a revolution, then landed on the other leg, the right back outside edge. But there was so much to remember: on the takeoff keep the left shoulder back, rotate counterclockwise, keep the right arm and shoulder back in the turn, keep the right leg close to the ice. And again, the challenge was to make three revolutions. Three! And Coach DiGregorio thought someday she might do a quad. Four revolutions!

Tara could see the moves in her mind, but she'd rather be making them on ice before a panel of judges. The dream was in front of her. The 1994 Winter Olympics would begin soon, and she could once again imagine that she was standing on the podium, holding flowers, with the National Anthem playing and a gold medal on a ribbon around her neck. Who knew what would happen in the 1998 games? She was aiming at 2002.

While Tara dreamed of Olympic glory, other skaters were being featured in lead stories on the TV news and making headlines in newspapers. A controversy at the U.S. National Figure Skating Championships, called the Nationals, would change the way the world viewed the sport.

On January 6, 1994, skater Nancy Kerrigan was clubbed on the right knee by an unknown attacker after a Nationals practice session at a rink in Detroit, Michigan.

Within a few days, a connection was made between the attacker and skater Tonya Harding, Nancy's toughest competitor for the national title. It was unclear just what Tonya knew about the plot, but later authorities found it was hatched by her ex-husband and a couple of his associates in an effort to get rid of Nancy and send Tonya to the Olympics. With no evidence at that time against Tonya, the USFSA let her skate in the competition. She won Nationals, giving her one of the two places on the Olympic team.

Nancy Kerrigan, the 1993 U.S. Ladies Figure Skating Champion, withdrew from the competition because of her knee injury. Doctors assured her that, with physical therapy, she could be skating again within a couple of weeks.

The Tonya Harding (above)–Nancy Kerrigan (below) controversy in the 1994 Olympics increased the American interest in figure skating.

As had happened on two other occasions in its history, the USFSA international committee voted to let an injured defending champion, because of her competitive record, have a spot on the U.S. Olympic team.

Tonya and Nancy represented the United States in the 1994 Lillehammer Olympics. Their rivalry garnered an unprecedented TV audience to watch them skate in the finals. Only three football Super Bowls had drawn more viewers.

The drama whetted Americans' appetites for figure skating. They wanted to see more of the exciting sport. In a survey, Americans ranked their favorite sport as football, followed by ladies figure skating, gymnastics, baseball, pairs figure skating, men's figure skating, and ice dancing. Four of the top seven sports were related to ice skating, and TV executives noticed.

The Olympic-style competitive skating that Tara practiced so hard was showcased on television annually during Nationals, Worlds, and every four years at the Olympics. And, former Olympic stars were skating in made-for-TV skating extravaganzas.

Was there room for both? The USFSA worried that show business skating with its emphasis on glitz and entertainment would steal the spotlight from Olympic-style skating, with its difficult required moves.

There was no amateur status among ice skaters. Those like Tara, who were seeking Olympic gold, could still skate for money, just like those skaters who had turned professional and no longer competed in ISU-sanctioned events.

Would the lure of show business steal some Olympic hopefuls from continuing along the road of practice, practice, practice between the few competitive events? Would some skaters rather hear the applause of crowds after easy jumps instead of enduring pre-dawn practice sessions in cold ice rinks working on difficult triples?

Tara never wavered from her goal. She was after Olympic gold. The way to get there was to practice with an eye toward national and world competitions. And practice was what she continued to do.

4

IN THE NEWS

Tara's determination and practice paid off. She placed second in the novice division at Nationals in 1994, and she found she thrived on competition.

By the summer of that year, Tara had mastered several triples and traveled to the U.S. Olympic Festival in St. Louis, Missouri. Just weeks after her 12th birthday, she won the gold medal and became the youngest first-place winner in the festival's history.

Reporters gathered around her after the big win. Here was a cute little girl—very talkative and what a jumper! Skating was still gaining popularity, and everyone wanted a story about tiny Tara Lipinski.

After the *New York Times* ran a long feature on her and her parents' sacrifices for her skat-

Tara skated in the novice division of the 1994 Nationals and placed second.

ing, TV networks jumped on the Tara bandwagon. Although a family living apart so that a child could train for the Olympics wasn't an oddity for skating or gymnastics, the Lipinskis became the poster family for devotion to a cause. ABC's *Good Morning America* interviewed her. TV news magazine *Prime Time Live* wanted to do a long segment on what it took to develop a gold medal figure skater.

Cameras followed Tara and her mother around. Tara skipped her tutoring session for the photo shoot and skated early and skated late for the *Prime Time Live* cameras. Her mother talked about the hardships this type of life involved.

Of course, there was the obvious financial burden of skating: travel to competitions (including airfare, meals, and hotels), entry fees, coaches' fees, skates and the sharpening of the blades every two and a half weeks, choreography fees, costumes, ballet lessons, ice time at the rink, and fees for mixing music for the programs. It all added up, and it added up fast. With the two separate households the Lipinskis kept—the house in Houston where Jack Lipinski lived and the family gathered for holidays and the apartment in Maryland where Pat and Tara lived—the costs were even higher. The Lipinskis estimated Tara's skating costs for 1994 were $58,000. It was a whopping amount just to learn competitive figure skating. Was the dream of Olympic gold worth it?

It was to Tara. Skating was her life.

And it was starting to pay off. In November she was asked to skate at "Ice Wars," a skating exhibition promoted by agent Mike Burg, who was talking to the Lipinskis about representing their daughter in the lucrative skating arena.

Other agents also called, but the Lipinskis made no deals for representation.

Because of her win at the Olympic Festival, Tara qualified for the junior Worlds competition in Budapest, Hungary, and there she placed fourth. That was excellent for a first-timer, but for Tara it wasn't enough.

She continued to practice. The 1995 junior Nationals loomed ahead, and she looked like a

Tara won the gold at the 1994 Olympic Festival and became the darling of the news media.

winner. But in the record books, winning the junior championship doesn't predict an Olympic winner. Few names of junior gold medalists are seen in the seniors' record book. If this is the stepping stone to the Olympics, the way of paying one's dues in front of the judges, then why don't more juniors go on to achieve greatness on the ice as seniors?

Most juniors are in their early teens, a time when their bodies begin to change with puberty. Sporadic weight gains, added inches in height, widening hips, and developing bust lines can interfere with a skater's jumping ability.

The singular devotion to skating in early years also takes its toll on some junior skaters. Some develop a life at school, outside the skating rink. Then there is the awakening interest in boys, which distracts young girls. Others can't cope with the pressures of moving into seniors. Skating burnout at 13 is not unheard of.

Another reason many juniors don't move to seniors is timing. Although there are national and world championships each year, the goal of an Olympic medal can't be reached year after year. A four-year training period stretches between Olympics, and it is four years filled with more expenses and more practice, practice, practice.

But Tara wasn't swayed. Sure, she was growing, but at a slow rate, and a doctor assured her that her small physique wasn't going to change drastically. She was 4 feet 5 inches tall now, and her adult height could reach 5 feet 1 inch, but probably no more than that. Her small frame was muscular enough to withstand the pressure of jumping.

As far as school went, she was doing fine under a tutor. Her social life was fairly confined to friends at the rink, and there weren't many boys there.

She was obsessed with skating. She practiced and practiced some more.

She was working hard on the flip jump. It was actually a toe-assisted Salchow. But timing on the takeoff was crucial. Her arm motion, placement of her toe on the ice, the rotation of her shoulders—all had to reach an end point at the same time for liftoff. She practiced again and again, and in the two and a half weeks before Nationals, she learned it and was able to land the triple.

The Axel was her hardest jump. It was named after the man who invented it, and a single Axel really meant one and a half rotations. So a double was two and a half, and a triple was three and a half. Take-off was from Tara's left forward outside edge, the rotation was counter-clockwise, and the landing was on her right back outside edge. She concentrated on getting it right.

In February of 1995, she traveled to Providence, Rhode Island, for the junior Nationals. The *Prime Time Live* cameras followed her. They needed a conclusion for their piece. A gold medal at Nationals would provide a great ending.

Tara's first practice was at 6:55 on a Sunday morning. Her coach, Jeff DiGregorio, watched her from judges' row, the place where coaches sit while their skaters practice. With him was Ron Ludington, the mentor of Delaware skaters. Megan Faulkner, Tara's coach from her Texas skating days, had traveled to Rhode Island to see her former student perform.

Two days later, Tara skated first in the short program. That position, determined by a drawing, isn't one skaters usually like. Judges nor-

Tara hit all her jumps in the short program and won the silver medal in the 1995 Junior Nationals.

mally hold a skater's scores down so they can give higher ones to a better skater later in the competition.

Wearing a black velvet dress and matching gloves, Tara skated well. She hit all her jumps. She nailed the triple loop–double loop combination and made the other mandatory movements in the short program look easy.

In "kiss and cry," the area where skaters wait with their coaches for their marks from the judges and kiss or cry according to what the marks warrant, she beamed her thousand-watt smile. Then came the technical marks, which ranged from 4.6 to 5.2, strong marks for juniors, but her artistic marks were lower. The judges had left room for other skaters to pass her.

Sydne Vogel from Alaska scored higher. At the end of the short programs, Tara was in second place. Still the media blitz continued. Newspapers the next day carried pictures of Tara and a mention of Sydne.

In the three-and-a-half-minute freestyle program, a half minute less than that required for senior skaters, Sydne Vogel skated in a red and gold costume to music from the musical *Les Miserables*. She started out with a bang, landing the triple Lutz, triple Salchow, triple flip, triple toe loop, and triple loop. Then her energy waned, and she fell on the difficult double Axel.

Still her marks were high. Technical scores ranged from 5.2 to 5.4, and for artistry she scored from 5.0 to 5.3.

Could Tara beat her?

Last in the long program, Tara skated to the song "Samson and Delilah." This time, she wore pink and pulled her brown hair back in a pony tail.

She darted onto the ice, but her first jump, a triple toe loop, looked a little shaky. From there she didn't make a mistake. She landed three combinations: double Axel–triple Salchow, triple loop–double loop, and triple Salchow–double toe loop. For the first time in competition, she tried a triple flip and landed it. For a grand finale, she hit a triple loop–double toe loop–double loop combination. What a performance!

Flowers and stuffed animals rained on the ice while applause surrounded her. In kiss and cry, she and her coach waited for her marks. Technical marks topped out at 5.5. But her artistic marks were again below Sydne Vogel's.

Tara Lipinski had won the silver medal, second place.

In the interview room after the awards, spunky Tara said, "I'll beat her next year."

It wasn't the finish that the reporters for *Prime Time Live* were looking for, but the 11-minute piece aired a few weeks later.

And talk in skating circles was of Tara moving up to seniors before the 1996 Nationals.

5
MOVING UP

For Tara, turning senior meant more work and more competition from seasoned veterans. She didn't expect to become a national champion in her first year, but that didn't keep her from giving all she had to each training session.

In competition she would face big stars, skaters she had admired and wanted to emulate, yet she needed to keep her own style. And her style was incredible. Because of her tiny size, she looked so perfect, so well-proportioned on the ice. She twirled and leaped and jumped, not far off the ice, but with tight spins that left audiences gasping.

And her athletic ability had reporters writing more and more stories about her. Because of so many requests for her to skate in exhibi-

Winning the silver medal in the 1995 Junior Nationals made Tara that much more eager to compete in the 1996 Senior Nationals.

tions and for interviews, Tara's parents hired agent Mike Burg to handle those details.

Tara wasn't the only skater with press clippings. With the skyrocketing popularity of figure skating, the public wanted to know more about skaters and their personalities.

Seventeen-year-old Nicole Bobek had been skating since she was three and a half years old, but unlike most skaters, she'd moved around a great deal. By the 1995 Nationals in Providence, Rhode Island, she'd had eight coaches in eight years. The last was esteemed coach Richard Callaghan of the Detroit Skating Club.

No one doubted Nicole's natural talent. With her blond hair and her charismatic style, she dazzled the skating world with her trademark spiral. But the spontaneous Nicole didn't like to practice. Nor did she like keeping training hours and eating healthy foods to keep her weight down. All those negatives added up to inconsistent skating.

Nicole's move to Detroit seemed to have a positive effect on her free spirit. She practiced regularly, and she ate right. Callaghan had insisted she train properly, and it paid off at Nationals.

The old lady of skating was Tonia Kwiatkowski. All of 23, she was a college graduate, a goal most skaters don't aspire to since academics often interfere with skating practice. Tonia was a late bloomer on the rink because, in her beginning years, practice sessions had been divided between spins and jumps and those compulsory tracings on ice. Once the school figures were dropped, she concentrated on the showy skating that earned a skater popular support and judges' points.

Youngest of the bunch and favored to finish first in the 1995 Nationals was Michelle Kwan. At 14, Michelle was viewed as the rising star of figure skating. The petite girl had been a year younger than Tara—12—when she moved to the seniors' division, but her story paralleled Tara's in many ways.

Michelle's family lived apart so that she and her sister Karen could train with a major coach. Her father lived in Torrance, a suburb of Los Angeles, while Michelle, her mother, and her sister lived at Lake Arrowhead, Calif., near the Ice Castles rink and her coach, Frank Carroll.

She also dropped out of public school and was privately tutored, squeezing her education into a two-and-a-half-hour period between her morning and afternoon skating sessions. She was the darling of the press, called an ice-queen-in-waiting because of her youth.

In 1994, Michelle had finished second at Nationals. Tonya Harding had won first, which gave her entry to the Olympics. With Nancy Kerrigan getting the nod to skate in the Olympics after the attack on her knee, and with the United States allowed only two skaters for the event, there was no space on the team for Michelle. Still, with Tonya's involvement in the attack unclear and knowing she would not be allowed to skate if she were legally indicted, the USFSA allowed Michelle to travel to Lillehammer, Norway, as an alternate for Tonya if needed. Michelle didn't get to skate in the Olympics, but she set her sights on the 1998 games.

Before the 1995 Nationals, Michelle was besieged by reporters with one question that cropped up time and again: the Jennifer Capriati question. Jennifer had turned tennis pro at age 13 with $5 million in endorsement contracts. Four years later, she was found in a Florida motel room using drugs with runaways. Was there such a thing as too much, too soon?

Michelle wasn't worried about that type of future. She felt she kept her world in balance by doing normal things, such as going to movies with friends. She enjoyed a happy family life, even though her father had to commute 200 miles to see her. Besides, she had no alternative if she wanted to skate competitively.

"To get that body in the air and make three turns, I'm afraid you've got to start them very young," her coach, Frank Carroll, told the press. "If you wait until they're 16 or 17, it's too late."

At the 1995 Nationals, where Tara won second in the juniors' division, the battle was on for a new seniors champ. After the short program, Tonia Kwiatkowski was first. Nicole Bobek claimed second, and Michelle Kwan was third.

The four-minute program would decide the winner. Here, artistry, emotion, and interpretation of the music were as important as the technical elements.

Tonia fell on one jump and was marked low in technical merit because her program wasn't as challenging as other skaters'. Michelle fell on her triple Lutz jump late in her program. Nicole, wearing a blue backless dress, skated a virtually error-free four minutes to music from the movie *Dr. Zhivago*. She landed five triple jumps cleanly and bobbled a sixth, but remained upright.

A new national champion was crowned. Nicole was first, Michelle was second, and Tonia came in third. All three headed to the 1995 Worlds in Birmingham, England. There, Nicole scored highest in the short program, but after the freestyle long program, the new champion of the world was Chen Lu of China. France's Surya Bonaly was second, leaving Nicole with the bronze medal for third. Although she skated the best performance of her life, Michelle Kwan came in fourth.

Figure skating judging is subjective, and there has been a long-standing deference to pecking order—allowing a skater to grow, wait her turn, and come back next year. Appearance was important, and Michelle, with minimal makeup and a ponytail, looked like a little girl on the ice while the other skaters appeared much more worldly. A more mature look was on Michelle's list of to-dos before next year's competitions.

Tara autographs a teddy bear for a member of one of her growing groups of fans and supporters.

These skaters dominated the national and world scene of ladies' figure skating, and now little Tara Lipinski was stepping up to their level of competition.

After Tara finished a disappointing fifth in the junior Worlds in Brisbane, Australia, rumor had it that Tara's mother and her coach, Jeff

DiGregorio, had a major disagreement. As Tara switched from juniors to seniors, she looked for a new coach.

A coach could make or break a skater. He or she was more than the person to hold on to in the kiss and cry area while waiting to hear marks after skating in competition. A coach was a mentor, a personal friend, and a stern taskmaster.

Tara and her mother set out on a three-week whirlwind tour interviewing coaches. Tara skated with Nicole Bobek's coach Richard Callaghan in Michigan. She visited Carol Heiss Jenkins, a former Olympic champion, who coached Tonia Kwiatkowski in Ohio. In Colorado, they talked with Kathy Casey. Galina Zmievskaia, who coached Olympians Viktor Petrenko and Oksana Baiul, was also in the running.

Kathy Casey was at the top of Tara and Patricia Lipinski's list, but before they could make the choice, Sydne Vogel signed with Casey.

Then Nicole Bobek announced she was leaving Detroit and Richard Callaghan. Now with a national title, Nicole had followed the lure of money. While most skaters practiced at their home rinks before the mid-January Nationals, she traveled much of December on the 16-city tour of "Nutcracker on Ice." Her coach traveled with her for afternoon training sessions, but mid-tour she decided to replace him with Coach Barbara Roles Williams of Las Vegas.

With Nicole's defection from Detroit, the Lipinskis jumped at the chance to work with Richard Callaghan. On Christmas Eve, they sealed the deal with Callaghan and flew home to celebrate Christmas in Texas, a family tradition.

Tara's father had decorated the house just like in the old days when they all lived together, using pictures from other Christmases as a guide. The family opened their gifts and celebrated together. On the morning of December 26, Tara and her mother climbed back on a plane for the 5 a.m. flight to Detroit.

While Tara practiced her short and long programs for her seniors debut, her mother looked around for a condo. It was nice that she found one that allowed dogs, since for three years Tara had been without her pets—Mischief, Coco, Brandy, Camelot, and Lancelot.

Tara took the changes—new coach, new home, and new seniors level—in stride. She was looking a few weeks ahead to Nationals and practiced with her normal determined air.

When asked about the upcoming competition, Tara said, "Even though I'm little, I have to skate like a woman. I'm just going to skate the best I can and see what happens. I'm not expecting a medal, but it would be nice."

"Some people have asked why I'd take Tara so close to Nationals," her new coach Richard Callaghan said. "She's self-disciplined. She's extremely talented. So, why not? If things go the way they should, Tara has a great future."

Tara practiced hard from the day after Christmas until it was time for the 1996 Nationals. Her freestyle program, designed by former pairs skater–turned–choreographer Lea Ann Miller, combined music from the soundtracks of two movies, *Speed* and *Prince of Tides.*

Finding the right music for a program is an art unto itself. The music needs dramatic peaks for the jumps; it needs slow, soothing sounds for the graceful spirals. Tara liked the

Choosing music that would showcase her artistic flare, Tara Lipinski skated her way into the 1996 World Championship.

Judges watched the skaters at practices so they could get a feel for what each skater could do.

music Miller chose, because it gave room for her technical moves and allowed artistry.

During competition week at Nationals, skaters rehearsed twice daily on a tightly run schedule. Several skaters were assigned the same time slot, so no skater had the ice alone. When Tara's music came on the loud speakers, she had the right of way in the rink. Other skaters practiced their jumps and twirls while Tara practiced her program. When another skater's music was played, Tara practiced her technical elements.

Practices were watched by judges, press members and fellow competitors. There were so many skaters to rank that judges needed this extra opportunity to witness what each skater could do. The judges set a range of scores so they would know how to spread their marks. They couldn't give high marks to the first few skaters and not leave an opportunity for more advanced skaters who performed near the end of the random line-up of the short program. Of course, the actual competition counted heavily, but judges were influenced by what they saw in practice too, and appearances were important. Tara dressed up for every session, wearing an appropriate skating costume as she prepared for the short program competition.

Defending U.S. National Figure Skating Champion Nicole Bobek was paying dearly for her decision to let training take a back seat to earning $90,000 for her Nutcracker tour. During one performance, she aggravated a tendon injury on the inside of her right ankle. The doctor told her she should take off two or three weeks to let it heal, but Nicole had signed a contract, and she fulfilled it.

Nor could she take off the two weeks prior to Nationals. She needed to train, to make up for time lost while on the road. Her new coach asked if Nicole could be awarded a bye onto the United States team that would compete at Worlds, but the president of USFSA suggested she show up and skate.

Once again the USFSA was going head to head with the exhibition circuit. The governing body understood the need for skaters to skate exhibitions to earn money to pay their exorbitant skating costs, but to choose show business over Olympic-style skating was frowned upon.

After the short programs were judged, it was no surprise that Michelle Kwan came out on top. Second was Tonia Kwiatkowski, and Nicole was third. Tara skated a good program but ranked fifth.

When it came time for the long programs, Nicole warmed up. Her ankle had felt better that morning, but had begun swelling in the afternoon. She had a doctor examine it. Minutes before her turn to skate, she withdrew from the competition.

Meanwhile, Michelle Kwan was skating the dance of the seven veils to three composers' interpretations of Salome, a Biblical character who danced for King Herod. With makeup and the dress of a harem woman, she looked the part. A year before, she had been criticized as looking too youthful. That was not a mistake she would repeat. Her performance was beguiling and mature. The judges gave her seven 5.9's and two 5.8's for artistic interpretation.

On the technical side, she landed seven triple jumps including a triple toe loop–triple toe loop combination, the only triple–triple combination in the ladies' competition.

Next to skate should have been Nicole, but Tara moved up in the schedule to fill the gap. She completed five triples and a triple Lutz–double toe loop combination, but she fell on a triple loop, which earned her marks from 5.4 to 5.8 on the technicals and gave her scores from 5.2 to 5.5 for artistry.

Tonia skated a sensational program with six triples and two combination jumps, a triple Lutz–double toe loop and a triple toe loop–double toe loop.

When the final scores were tallied, Michelle was the new Nationals champion, Tonia was second, and little Tara had earned third place in her first competition as a senior.

As the winner, Michelle was assured a place on the U.S. team that would go to the Worlds. The other two members were decided by USFSA committee. Normally the silver and bronze medalists would be named to the team, but Nicole had asked for a bye as the defending Nationals champion. Should the committee bump Tara off the team and let Nicole compete? The committee had given Nancy Kerrigan a medical exemption and named her to the Olympic team, and precedent had been set, but this time the committee said no to a returning champ.

Their message was clear. Exhibition skating was not more important than USFSA-sanctioned events. As former Olympic gold medalist Scott Hamilton summed it up, "You can't put a price on winning a World or Olympic title. It gives you credibility for life."

Tara Lipinski was going to the Worlds.

In Edmonton, Canada, in March 1996, Tara represented the United States against the world's best skaters. Although at 13 she was the youngest in the competition, she handled press interviews like a pro.

In 1996, Tara won a silver medal in the Skate Canada competition, one of the six Champion Series events.

When asked what she did in her spare time, she answered, "I have a normal life. I'm in eighth grade. I have my friends over on weekends, we do sleepovers and things like that."

Normal for a skater, maybe, but not many eighth graders had three tutors. One taught her algebra and geometry, another worked with her on Spanish, and a third tutored her in social studies, science, and English. And not many eighth graders got to travel internationally.

Awed by the skating talent around her, Tara

concentrated on her technical elements in the short program, but she fell twice. Only 24 skaters would make it through that qualifying round and be allowed to skate the long freestyle program. When all competitors had completed their short programs, Tara ranked 23rd.

She would skate in the long program.

Dressed in red, she darted around the ice, a smile on her face. She was here to have fun and seemed more relaxed than in the earlier program. She landed seven triple jumps and at the end of her four minutes, she waved her hands over her head at the crowd, which gave her a thunderous standing ovation.

The 1996 World Champion was Michelle Kwan, who executed seven triple jumps and narrowly beat China's Chen Lu, the defending champion, who completed six triples. In third was Irina Slutskaya of Russia. Tara was ranked 15th, an excellent finish for the youngest skater.

But was she content with that? For a few minutes. Then she focused on doing better next year.

Work began on new programs, and Tara also allowed time to skate a few exhibitions. Although the family still kept two homes, one in Texas and one in Michigan, which was a financial drain, Tara's skating was now paying its own way.

The six Champions Series qualifying competitions began, and Tara received invitations to participate. At the International Skating Union's fall competition at Skate Canada, she ranked third after the short program. In the long program she executed three jump combinations, including a triple Salchow–triple loop, which won her the silver medal.

Five days later she stepped up to the podium in Paris, France, to receive the bronze medal at Trophy Lalique. She stayed in Europe for the Nations Cup in Germany as a replacement in the U.S. delegation for injured Nicole Bobek and won another silver medal.

The three medals earned her one of the six spots for ladies figure skaters at the finals scheduled for early 1997 in Hamilton, Ontario, Canada.

During a breather before the 1997 competitions began, Tara skated at an exhibition in Long Beach, California. One of the sponsors of the event was donating a great deal of money to The City of Hope, a hospital and research center for children with cancer and other serious illnesses. With the donation came a request for a skater to visit the hospital. Tara volunteered. What she found there touched her heart.

One boy told her he was having a bad day. That was a phrase Tara had used many times in her life to describe days when her skating lacked its usual sparkle. Here was a boy fighting for his life and having a really bad day. That remark put her skating in perspective.

But she didn't lose her drive to win Olympic gold. That goal remained, as it had since she had first donned ice skates. Now, though, she felt compelled to help others, to give something back, because she had so much.

If her presence could cheer up others, then she would go to hospitals whenever her schedule allowed.

Next stop was Vanderbilt Children's Hospital a few days before the February 1997 Nationals in Nashville. Tara took time from her busy schedule to give valentines to the kids.

Tara's goal at the 1997 Nationals was to be in the top three and win a place on the team that skated at the Worlds. Beating Michelle Kwan, who had won nine Olympic-style competitions in a row in the previous 11 months, didn't seem a possibility.

Now at 14, Tara continued to practice. She increased her ballet time, aiming for grace and poise and a more mature look. Her new short program, ironically set to music from the soundtrack of the movie *Little Women*, included the difficult triple Lutz–double loop combination and a triple flip.

When, at the end of the short program, she ranked second behind Michelle, Tara was elated. Now if she could skate a clean long program, she would be assured of a chance to skate at the Worlds.

Tara proudly won the 1997 World Figure Skating Championship as part of the United States team. Here she skates in the Parade of Champions.

Nicole Bobek, who had changed coaches yet again, this time to Carlo Fassi, skated a crowd-pleasing long program to music from the ballet *Giselle*. She attempted only four triple jumps but landed them all.

Michelle started her program with a lovely triple Lutz–double toe loop. She landed the first part of her next combination jump, a triple toe loop–triple toe loop, then fell hard to the ice. She seemed stunned, and panic took control. On her next jump she stumbled, and on the following one she fell again. She regained a portion of her former confidence and finished her program.

Michelle's disastrous long program gave Tara a chance at the gold.

Choreographer Sandra Bezic's artistic touch was apparent in Tara's freestyle program. Wearing a ballerina-style white dress and skating to music from the soundtracks of *Sense and Sensibility* and *Much Ado About Nothing*, Tara leaped, twirled, spiraled, and skated the best program of her life. She hit seven triples.

Midway through her program, she became the first ladies skater to land a combination triple loop–triple loop in competition. The crowd rose to its feet. The roar didn't stop until after Tara completed her last spin. Flowers rained from the stands and covered the ice.

Tara rewrote history and became the youngest National Champion, replacing Sonya Klopfer, who won at 15 in 1951.

In the press room after her triumph, Tara said, "I'm in shock. I'm on a different wave length. Something high."

Coach Callaghan took a pragmatic approach to the victory. "I think Tara is bright enough to accept she had a great night, and the champion

Tara hit seven triple jumps in her freestyle program at the '97 Nationals and became the first woman skater to land a combination triple loop–triple loop in competition.

had a bad night. Tara has a lot of years left, and she will have highs and lows."

But what a high!

Her picture hit the front pages of newspapers. Requests for interviews and guest appearances on TV shows poured in. In a whirlwind Monday in New York, Tara taped an interview for *CBS This Morning* then sat through a live interview on *Good Morning, America.* She was glad the men's National Champion, Todd Elderedge, was also there. Coach Callaghan had coached them both to gold medals.

Would a trip to New York be complete with-

Tara displayed her artistic and athletic ability and skated the best program of her life at the 1997 Nationals, making women's figure skating history in the process.

out watching a taping of David Letterman's *Late Show*? Since Tara was one of his biggest fans, she convinced her mom to go to the Ed Sullivan Theater, where she got to visit backstage in the green room with guests awaiting their turns to go on stage. After the show she met Dave himself. What a thrill for a 14-year-old!

Tara's new management team, Edge Marketing, created a web page, Tara's Place, so her fans could keep up with her activities. Her site at www.taralipinski.com was up and running shortly after her big win as the U.S. National Figure Skating Champion.

But there were more competitions ahead, so Tara turned down other interview opportunities to train for the Champions Series Finals. She was one of six skaters who qualified for the international event held in Hamilton, Ontario, Canada. And one of the others was Michelle Kwan.

Was Tara's victory at Nationals a fluke? Or was she capable of beating the World Champion again?

When the skating was over, Michelle Kwan had a decent night, but Tara scored one-tenth of a point higher, and that was all it took for her to win the gold once again.

Tara's sights had been set on the 2002 Olympics, but with these wins, was there hope for the 1998 Olympics in Nagano, Japan?

The Worlds in Switzerland loomed ahead, and with her mind focused not on winning but on performing her best, she once again proved that her tiny frame could make those jumps and still be graceful doing it.

At Worlds Michelle Kwan, her confidence lacking, still struggled with what she called her coma period. Was she a victim of age? Had her maturing body betrayed her? With the grace she showed on the ice, she accepted the silver medal beside Tara, who had landed on top of the world.

At 14, Tara was the youngest-ever World Figure Skating Champion! Now what?

Tara Lipinski would be in the record books. With the minimum age limit now set at 15, no one her age would be allowed to compete in the Worlds again, so the record would stand permanently.

Tara (center) won gold again at the 1997 World Figure Skating Championship in Switzerland. Michelle Kwan (left) took silver and Vanessa Gusmeroli took bronze.

The International Skating Union had come under fierce criticism for turning the sport into a young girls' jumping contest. When Sonja Henie won three Olympic gold medals from 1927 to 1936, her most difficult jump was a single Axel. In the 1976 Olympics, Dorothy Hamill won gold with a double Axel as her most impressive jump. Tara won the Worlds title with seven triples, and her coach was talking about quads.

This was ladies' figure skating. Where were the ladies? The 1994 Olympic gold winner was 16; the defending World Champion had won her title at 15; the new World Champion was 14. Jumps required small and thin physiques, strong enough to jump high, but light enough to spin quickly. Figure skating was being compared to gymnastics, where anyone over 13 and 90 pounds was considered a has-been and overweight.

Eating disorders were the norm, and burnout from coaches' high expectations were commonplace. Pressures from a high-profile life overwhelmed many skaters. Would Tara face these problems, too?

Right now she could eat what she wanted without gaining weight, and that included pizza and chocolate chip cookie dough ice cream. But she limited those foods and normally ate pastas and healthy fruits and vegetables.

She loved skating and practice. Her coach said he had to pull in the reins on her. At practices she watched the male skaters and wanted to do all they could do. She pushed herself, instead of being pushed by her parents or her coach.

And she enjoyed the attention the press was giving her. She'd been a guest on David Letterman's show and also on Rosie O'Donnell's talk show. Her file of press clippings continued to grow.

During the summer of 1997, she crisscrossed the United States with the Campbell's Soups Tour of World Figure Skating Champions, earning a staggering amount of money that would pay her skating expenses for years to come. Although the 59-city tour cut into her practice time, she concentrated on artistry and facial expressions while she skated in arenas full of spectators.

Between shows in Wisconsin and Minneso-

Winning the gold medal at the 1997 Worlds caused Tara to change her goal of winning Olympic gold in the year 2002 to winning Olympic gold in 1998!

ta, Tara turned 15. While traveling from city to city on the tour bus, she did her homework or slept or talked with other skaters, including Michelle Kwan.

Tara Lipinski began her skating career with one goal in mind: an Olympic gold medal. She was ahead of schedule. Instead of 2002, she would first focus on the 1998 Olympics.

What would the future hold for this promising young athlete?

"She's going to college," her mother said. "She promised me."

Tara would like to be a lawyer, but whatever Tara puts her mind to, her determination and ability to focus on a goal will likely take her far.

CHRONOLOGY

1982 Born to Patricia and Jack Lipinski in Philadelphia, Pa., on June 10; lives in Sewell, N.J.

1985 Learns to roller skate.

1988 Tries ice skating for the first time.

1991 Moves to Sugar Land, Texas, where father becomes a vice president for Coastal Corporation, an energy company.

1993 Moves back East with mother to train at University of Delaware under coach Jeff DiGregorio.

1994 Wins U.S. Olympic Festival (St. Louis, Mo.); places fourth in World Figure Skating Championships junior competition (Budapest, Hungary).

1995 Places second in U.S. National Figure Skating Championships junior competition (Providence, R.I.); places fifth in World Figure Skating Championships junior competition (Brisbane, Australia); advances to senior level competition; moves to Bloomfield Hills, Mich., to train with coach Richard Callaghan.

1996 Places third in U.S. National Figure Skating Championships (San Jose, Ca.); places fifteenth in World Figure Skating Championships (Edmonton, Alberta, Canada); places second in Skate Canada (Kitchner, Ontario, Canada), third in Trophy Lalique (Paris, France), and second in Nations Cup (Gelsenkirchen, Germany), all in the Champions Series.

1997 Wins U.S. National Figure Skating Championship (Nashville, Tenn.); Wins Finals in Champions Series (Hamilton, Ontario, Canada); Wins World Figure Skating Championship (Lausanne, Switzerland); Tours with Campbell's Soups Tour of World Figure Skating Champions.

SUGGESTIONS FOR FURTHER READING

Bezic, Sandra. *The Passion to Skate: An Intimate View of Figure Skating.* Atlanta: Turner Publishing, Inc., 1996.

Berman, Alice. *Skater's Edge Sourcebook.* Kensington, Md.: Skater's Edge, 1995.

Brennan, Christine. *Inside Edge: A Revealing Journey into the Secret World of Figure Skating.* New York: Scribner, 1996.

Donohue, Shiobhan. *Kristi Yamaguchi: Artist on Ice.* Minneapolis, Minn.: Lerner, 1993.

Gutman, Dan. *Ice Skating from Axels to Zambonis.* New York: Viking, 1995.

Kerrigan, Nancy and Woodward, Steve. *Nancy Kerrigan: In My Own Words.* New York: Hyperion, 1996.

Petkevich, John Misha. *Sports Illustrated Figure Skating Championship Techniques.* New York: Time, Inc., 1989.

Smith, Beverly. *Figure Skating: A Celebration.* New York, NY: St. Martin's Press, 1994.

Swift, E.M. "Kid Stuff." *Sports Illustrated*, February 24, 1997, pp. 28-31.

ABOUT THE AUTHOR

Award-winning writer Veda Boyd Jones enjoys the challenge of writing for a variety of readers. Her published works include eight adult novels, two children's historical novels, a coloring book, and numerous articles and short stories in national magazines. In addition to working at her computer, she teaches writing and speaks at writers' conferences. Mrs. Jones lives in Missouri with her husband Jimmie, an architect, and three sons.

INDEX

PICTURE CREDITS
AP/Wide World Photos: 2, 6, 8, 10, 12, 18, 41, 52, 58, 60; photo © J. Barry Mittan:17, 20, 26 (above), 26 (below), 29, 31, 34, 36, 44, 46, 49, 55, 56.